People In High Office

Monarch - George VI

British Prime Minister
26th July 1945
- 26th October 1951

U.S. President
12th April 1945
- 20th January 1953

Clement Attlee
Labour Party

Harry S. Truman
Democratic Party

Australia

Prime Minister
Ben Chifley

Brazil

President
Eurico Gaspar Dutra

Canada

Prime Minister
William Lyon Mackenzie King

1946 U.K.

YEARBOOK

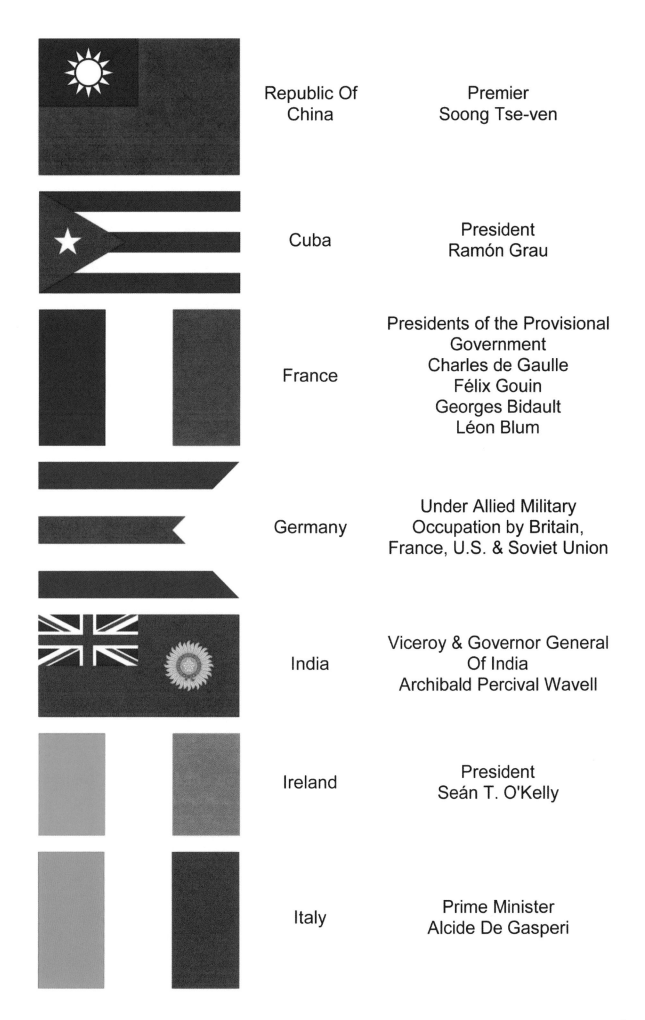

Republic Of China	Premier Soong Tse-ven	
Cuba	President Ramón Grau	
France	Presidents of the Provisional Government Charles de Gaulle Félix Gouin Georges Bidault Léon Blum	
Germany	Under Allied Military Occupation by Britain, France, U.S. & Soviet Union	
India	Viceroy & Governor General Of India Archibald Percival Wavell	
Ireland	President Seán T. O'Kelly	
Italy	Prime Minister Alcide De Gasperi	

Japan

Under Allied Occupation
Prime Ministers
Kijūrō Shidehara
Shigeru Yoshida

Mexico

Presidents
Manuel Ávila Camacho
Miguel Alemán Valdés

New Zealand

Prime Minister
Peter Fraser

Spain

President
Francisco Franco

South Africa

Prime Minister
Jan Smuts

Soviet Union

Communist Party Leader
Joseph Stalin

Turkey

Prime Ministers
Şükrü Saracoğlu
Recep Peker

EVENTS FROM 1946

JANUARY

1st   London's Heathrow Airport had its first international flight flying to Buenos Aires, Argentina. (At the time Heathrow was called London Airport - it was renamed Heathrow Airport in 1966).

1st   The UK's Atomic Energy Research Establishment is established at Harwell near Oxford.

17th   The United Nations Security Council holds its first meeting at Church House, Westminster in London.

FEBRUARY

14th   The Bank of England is nationalised.

15th   It is reported that the American dance craze the Jitterbug has started to sweep Britain.

20th   Royal Opera House in Covent Garden re-opens after the War with The Royal Ballet (relocated from Sadler's Wells Theatre) performing The Sleeping Beauty.

A couple dancing the Jitterbug at the Paramount Dance Hall on Tottenham Court Road.

MARCH

5th	Winston Churchill delivers his "Iron Curtain" speech at Westminster College in Fulton, Missouri, United States.
9th	33 people are killed and hundreds injured at the Bolton Wanderers stadium disaster at Burnden Park, Bolton.
10th	British troops begin withdrawal from Lebanon.
24th	BBC Home Service radio broadcasts Alistair Cooke's first American Letter.

Alistair Cooke reported on America for the BBC for 58 years. He completed his 2,869th weekly Letter From America in 2004 just weeks before his death from cancer at the age of 95. The series was the longest-running speech radio programme in history.

APRIL

27th	The first post-war FA Cup final is won by Derby County who beat Charlton Athletic 4-1 at Wembley Stadium.

MAY

4th	First-class cricket returns having been suspended during the War.
20th	The House of Commons votes to nationalise coal mines in the United Kingdom.
23rd	Terence Rattigan's drama The Winslow Boy premieres in London.
31st	London Airport was officially opened for commercial operations.

Early photos of London Airport (Heathrow) when its passenger terminals were just tents.

JUNE

1st   The television licence is introduced and a black and white TV licence will now costs £2 per annum.

7th   After being suspended during World War II BBC Television resumes broadcasting.

8th   A victory parade is held in London to celebrate the end of the War.

28th   The government imposes bread rationing.

The London Victory Celebrations were British Commonwealth, Empire and Allied victory celebrations held after the defeat of Nazi Germany and Japan in World War II. The celebrations consisted mainly of a military parade through the city and a night time fireworks display. All the allies were represented at the parade except for the USSR, Yugoslavia and Poland.

JULY

15th   Homeless families squat in a former Army camp at Scunthorpe.
A 13 coach express train hurtled of the rails at Hatfield, Herts miraculously leaving only 11 injured.

AUGUST

1st   Communist Party member Arthur Horner becomes General Secretary of the National Union of Mineworkers.
The Finance Act receives Royal Assent which includes the establishment of the National Land Fund to secure culturally significant property for the nation as a memorial to the dead of WW II.

6th   Family allowance introduced.

6th   A daily free ⅓ pint of milk is to be provided in UK state schools to all pupils under the age of 18.

9th   The Arts Council is incorporated by Royal Charter.

31st   League football returns after having been suspended during the War.

SEPTEMBER

The Britain Can Make It exhibition at the Victoria and Albert Museum in London is promoted by the Council of Industrial Design and the Board of Trade to show off good domestic and industrial design.

8th   A mass squat by homeless families in London is organised by the Communist Party.

15th   The Marshal of the Royal Air Force Sir Arthur Harris, Commander-in-Chief of RAF Bomber Command, retires.

16th   Popular quiz show Have a Go! with Wilfred Pickles makes its first national broadcast on BBC Radio.

29th   BBC Light Programme begins broadcasting. It was the third national radio network broadcast by the BBC, the other two being the Home Service (mainly speech-based) and the Light Programme, principally devoted to light entertainment and music. The Third Programme became BBC Radio 3 in April 1970.

Queues outside the Victoria and Albert Museum for the Britain Can Make It exhibition.

OCTOBER

1st   J. B. Priestley's drama, An Inspector Calls starring Ralph Richardson, premieres at the New Theatre, London.

7th   The BBC Light Programme transmits the first episodes of the daily radio magazine programme Woman's Hour and also the daily adventure serial Dick Barton - Special Agent. In the years to follow BBC Light Programme would go on to produce a host of stars including Ted Ray, Donald Peers, Tony Hancock, Frankie Howerd, Max Bygraves, Archie Andrews, Peter Brough and the Goons.

NOVEMBER

1st   The premiere of the Powell and Pressburger film, A Matter of Life and Death starring David Niven, becomes the First Royal Command Performance at a public cinema (at the Empire, Leicester Square).

10th   Peter Scott opens the Slimbridge Wetland Reserve in Gloucestershire.

NOVEMBER

11th	Stevenage, a village in Hertfordshire, is designated by the Attlee government as Britain's first new town to relieve overcrowding and replace bombed homes in London. The new town is set to have around 60,000 residents once it is completed with the first homes expected to be ready by 1952 and the town to be fully developed by the early 1960s. The town's centrepiece will be a revolutionary pedestrianised central shopping area.
17th	Eight British Army servicemen are killed in Jerusalem by Jewish terrorists.
22nd	Tony Benn is elected as Treasurer of the Oxford Union.
29th	The world's first regular half-hour situation comedy, Pinwright's Progress, premieres on BBC Television.

DECEMBER

22nd	The milk ration is increased from 2 to 2½ pints per week.
26th	David Lean's film of Great Expectations, based on the novel by Charles Dickens, is released.

Still from Great Expectations with Miss Havisham (Martita Hunt), Young Estella (Jean Simmons) and Young Pip (Tony Wager). The film won two Academy Awards (Best Art Direction and Best Cinematography) and was nominated for three others (Best Picture, Best Director and Best Screenplay).

OTHER EVENTS FROM 1946

- Cinema going reaches an all-time peak with 1,635 million admissions during the whole of 1946.
- There is a lifting of prohibition on married women working in the Civil Service.
- Fred Pontin's first holiday camp at Brean Sands, Burnham-on-Sea, Somerset is opened.
- The University of Bristol establishes the first university drama department in the UK.
- The best-selling Bush DAC90 bakelite radio introduced.

The crowds at the Warner West End cinema (now Vue Leicester Square), London, 1946.

UK PERSONALITIES

BORN IN 1946

John Baldwin
3rd January 1946

Multi-instrumentalist, songwriter, composer, arranger and record producer better known by his stage name John Paul Jones. Baldwin was the bassist, keyboardist and co-songwriter for the rock band Led Zeppelin. A versatile musician he plays organ, guitar, koto, lap steel guitars, mandolin, autoharp, violin, ukulele, sitar, cello, continuum and recorder.

Roger Keith "Syd" Barrett
6th January 1946 –
7th July 2006

Barrett was a musician, composer, singer, songwriter and painter. Best known as a founder member of the band Pink Floyd, Barrett was the lead singer, guitarist and principal songwriter in its early years and is credited with naming the band. Barrett was excluded from Pink Floyd in April 1968 after David Gilmour took over as their new frontman.

Julian Patrick Barnes
19th January 1946

A writer, Barnes won the Man Booker Prize for his book The Sense of an Ending (2011). Three of his earlier books had also been shortlisted for the Booker Prize: Flaubert's Parrot (1984), England, England (1998) and Arthur & George (2005). He has also written crime fiction under the pseudonym Dan Kavanagh and in 2004 he became a Commandeur of L'Ordre des Arts et des Lettres. His other honours include the Somerset Maugham Award and the Geoffrey Faber Memorial Prize.

Peter William "Pete" Postlethwaite, OBE
7th February 1946 –
2nd January 2011

Actor and former drama teacher who after minor television appearances, including in The Professionals had his first big success with the 1988 film Distant Voices, Still Lives. Director Steven Spielberg called him "the best actor in the world" after working with him on The Lost World: Jurassic Park. He was nominated for an Academy Award for Best Supporting Actor for In the Name of the Father in 1993 and was made an OBE in the 2004 New Year Honours list.

Clare Short
15th February 1946

Politician and a member of the Labour Party, Short was the MP for Birmingham Ladywood from 1983 to 2010. For most of this period she was a Labour Party MP until she resigned the party whip in 2006 and served the remainder of her term as an Independent. Short served as Secretary of State for International Development in the government of Prime Minister Tony Blair from the 3rd May 1997 until her resignation from that post on the 12th May 2003.

Arthur Ian Lavender
16th February 1946

Stage, film and television actor better known as Ian Lavender. His best known role is as Private Pike in the BBC comedy series Dad's Army. Following the death of Clive Dunn in 2012 he is the last surviving cast member to have played a character in the platoon. More recently he has continued with his stage career and played the role of Derek Harkinson in Eastenders.

Brenda Anne Blethyn, OBE
20th February 1946

Actress who has worked in theatre, television and film and is best known for her role in Mike Leigh's drama Secrets & Lies. Blethyn has received two Academy Award nominations and three Golden Globe Award nominations, winning one (1996). In addition she has won a BAFTA, an Empire Award, a Golden Lion, a Theatre World Award, a Critics' Circle Theatre Award and a Laurence Olivier Award nomination for her theatrical work.

Alan Sidney Patrick Rickman
21st February 1946

Rickman is a former member of the Royal Shakespeare Company in both modern and classical theatre productions. His breakout performance was his 1985 role as the Vicomte de Valmont in the play Les Liaisons Dangereuses for which he was nominated for a Tony Award. Rickman is well known for his film performances as the Sheriff of Nottingham in Robin Hood: Prince of Thieves for which he won the BAFTA Award and Severus Snape in the Harry Potter film series.

Robert Finlayson Cook
28th February 1946 –
6th August 2005

Labour Party politician who studied at the University of Edinburgh before becoming a Member of Parliament for Edinburgh Central in 1974. Cook then served as the MP for Livingston from 1983 until his death and was in the Cabinet as Foreign Secretary from 1997 to 2001. In parliament he was known for his debating ability which saw his rise through the political ranks.

David Jon Gilmour, CBE
6th March 1946

Musician, singer, songwriter and multi-instrumentalist. In a career spanning more than 50 years he is best known for his work as the guitarist and co-lead vocalist of the progressive rock band Pink Floyd. It was estimated that by 2012 the group had sold over 250 million records worldwide including 75 million units sold in the United States.

Timothy Peter Dalton
21st March 1946

Actor who is best known for portraying James Bond in The Living Daylights (1987) and Licence to Kill (1989). He is also known for playing Rhett Butler in the television mini-series Scarlett (1994) and Sir Malcolm Murray on the television series Penny Dreadful (2014–present).

Susan Lillian "Sue" Townsend, FRSL
2nd April 1946 –
10th April 2014

Writer and humourist whose work encompasses novels, plays and works of journalism. She was best known for creating the character Adrian Mole with which she enjoyed great success in the 1980s selling more books than any other work of fiction in Britain during that decade. Both the earliest Adrian Mole book and The Queen and I (1992) were adapted for the stage and enjoyed successful runs in London's West End.

Thomas Leslie "Les" Gray
9th April 1946 –
21st February 2004

Musician best known for his work with glam rock pop band Mud. Mud had a string of hits written by Nicky Chinn and Mike Chapman including two which topped the UK Singles Chart in 1974, "Lonely This Christmas" and "Tiger Feet". Gray was also known for his distinctive vocal impersonation of Elvis Presley.

Timothy James "Tim" Curry
19th April 1946

Actor and singer known for his work in a diverse range of theatre, film and television productions, often portraying villainous roles or character parts. Curry first rose to prominence with his portrayal of Dr Frank-N-Furter in the 1975 cult film The Rocky Horror Picture Show reprising the role he had originated in the 1973 London and 1974 Los Angeles stage productions of The Rocky Horror Show.

Joanna Lamond Lumley, OBE
1st May 1946

Actress, voice-over artist, former model, author and activist who starred in the British television series Absolutely Fabulous as Edina Monsoon's best friend, Patsy Stone, as well as in The New Avengers, Sapphire & Steel, Jam & Jerusalem and Sensitive Skin. In film she has appeared in On Her Majesty's Secret Service (1969), Trail of the Pink Panther (1982) and James and the Giant Peach (1996).

John Marshall Watson, MBE
4th May 1946

Former racing driver and commentator from Northern Ireland. He competed in Formula One winning five Grands Prix and also in the World Sportscar Championship. After his retirement from motorsport he became a commentator for Eurosport's coverage of Formula One from 1990 to 1996. He currently commentates on the Blancpain GT Series.

Donovan Philips Leitch
10th May 1946

Singer, songwriter and guitarist better. He developed an eclectic and distinctive style that blended folk, jazz, pop, psychedelia, and world music (notably calypso). Emerging from the British folk scene Donovan reached fame in the United Kingdom in early 1965 with live performances on the pop TV series, Ready Steady Go!. Some of his most successful singles include Catch the Wind, Colours, Mellow Yellow and Hurdy Gurdy Man.

Maureen Diane Lipman, CBE
10th May 1946

Film, theatre and television actress, columnist and comedienne. Lipman first gained prominence on television in the 1979 situation comedy Agony as an agony aunt with a troubled private life. She was awarded the Laurence Olivier Theatre Award for Best Comedy Performance in 1985 for See How They Run and has continued to work in the theatre for over thirty years playing, amongst other roles, Aunt Eller in the National Theatre's Oklahoma! with Hugh Jackman.

George Best
22nd May 1946 –
25th November 2005

Professional footballer who played as a winger for Manchester United and the Northern Ireland national team. In 1968 he won the European Cup with United, was named the European Footballer of the Year and FWA Footballer of the Year. He has been described by the Irish Football Association as the "greatest player to ever pull on the green shirt of Northern Ireland".

Neville John "Noddy" Holder, MBE
15th June 1946

Musician and actor. Holder was the lead vocalist and guitarist with the rock band Slade who had numerous hits in the 1970s and 80s. Holder co-wrote most of Slade's material with bassist Jim Lea. Slade are best remembered for the single "Merry Xmas Everybody" with the song becoming the band's sixth number one. "Merry Xmas Everybody" has remained an extremely popular festive classic with UK sales alone reaching several million copies.

John Whitaker "Jack" Straw
3rd August 1946

Politician who served as the MP for Blackburn from 1979 to 2015. Straw served in the Cabinet from 1997 to 2010 under the governments of Tony Blair and Gordon Brown. Under Blair he held two of the traditional Great Offices of State, Home Secretary from 1997 to 2001 and Foreign Secretary from 2001 to 2006. Throughout Brown's Premiership he served as Lord Chancellor and the Secretary of State for Justice.

Keith John Moon
23rd August 1946 –
7th September 1978

Drummer who played with the rock band The Who. He was noted for his unique style and his eccentric, often self-destructive behaviour. His drumming continues to be praised by critics and musicians. He was posthumously inducted into the Modern Drummer Hall of Fame in 1982 becoming only the second rock drummer to be chosen and in 2011 Moon was voted the second-greatest drummer in history by a Rolling Stone readers' poll.

Alison Steadman, OBE
26th August 1946

As an actress Steadman received BAFTA TV Award nominations for the 1986 BBC serial The Singing Detective and for the ITV drama series Fat Friends (2001). In 1991 she won the National Society of Film Critics Award for Best Actress for the Mike Leigh film Life is Sweet and then in 1993 the Olivier Award for Best Actress for her role as Mari in the original production of The Rise and Fall of Little Voice.

Barry Alan Crompton Gibb, CBE
1st September 1946

Singer, songwriter, instrumentalist and producer who rose to worldwide fame as the founder of the pop music group the Bee Gees. One of the most commercially successful groups in the history of popular music, Gibb's career has spanned over fifty years. In 1994 he was inducted into the Songwriters Hall of Fame with his brothers and in 1997, as a member of the Bee Gees, he was inducted into the Rock and Roll Hall of Fame and received the Brit Award for Outstanding Contribution to Music.

Michael "Mike" Bull,
OBE
11th September 1946

Retired pole vaulter and decathlete. Bull first achieved success at the 1966 Commonwealth Games winning a silver medal in the pole vault. At later Commonwealth Games he went on to win two gold medals, one in the pole vault (1970) and the other in the decathlon (1974). He appeared in 69 internationals for Great Britain and captained the Great Britain and Northern Ireland teams on numerous occasions. In 1991 he won the World Masters pole vault in Finland.

Felicity Ann Kendal,
CBE
25th September 1946

Television and theatre actress. Kendal has appeared in numerous stage and screen roles over her 45-year career but the role that gave her big break on television was the BBC sitcom The Good Life (1975-1978). Starring alongside Richard Briers, as Barbara and Tom Good, they played a middle-class suburban couple who decide to quit the rat race and become self-sufficient much to the consternation of their snooty but well-meaning neighbours.

Edwina Jones
13th October 1946

More commonly known by her first married name Edwina Currie she is the former MP for South Derbyshire. First elected as a Conservative Party MP in 1983 she was a Junior Health Minister for two years before resigning in 1988 over the controversy regarding salmonella in eggs. After losing her seat in 1997 she began a new career as a novelist and broadcaster. She is the author of six novels and has also written four works of non-fiction.

Janet Street-Porter
27th December 1946

Celebrity, media personality, journalist and broadcaster. She was the editor, for two years, of The Independent on Sunday but relinquished the job to become editor-at-large in 2002. She has made numerous television appearances on programmes such Question Time, I'm a Celebrity... Get Me Out of Here!, Celebrity MasterChef and Have I Got News for You. Since 2011 she has been a regular panellist on the ITV lifestyle and chat show Loose Women.

Marianne Evelyn Faithfull
29th December 1946

Singer, songwriter and actress whose career has spanned six decades. Her early work in pop and rock music in the 1960s was overshadowed by her struggle with drug abuse in the 1970s. After a long commercial absence she returned late in 1979 with the highly acclaimed album Broken English. Faithfull's subsequent solo work, often critically acclaimed, has at times been overshadowed by her personal history.

TOP 10
SINGLES 1946

No.1	Frank Sinatra	Five Minutes More
No.2	Perry Como	Prisoner Of Love
No.3	Nat King Cole	(I Love You) For Sentimental Reasons
No.4	Vaughn Monroe	Let It Snow! Let It Snow! Let It Snow!
No.5	The Ink Spots	Bless You (For Being An Angel)
No.6	Bing Crosby & The Jesters	Sioux City Sue
No.7	Johnny Mercer	Personality
No.8	Eddy Howard	To Each His Own
No.9	Dinah Shore	Gypsy
No.10	Frankie Carle & His Orchestra	Oh! What It Seemed To Be

① Frank Sinatra
Five Minutes More

Label:	Written by:	Length:
Columbia	Jule Cahn / Sammy Styne	2 mins 38 secs

Francis Albert "Frank" Sinatra (12th December 1915 - 14th May 1998) was a singer, actor, director and producer. Sinatra is one of the best-selling music artists of all time having sold more than 150 million records worldwide. He was awarded the Presidential Medal of Freedom by Ronald Reagan in 1985 and the Congressional Gold Medal in 1997. Sinatra was also the recipient of eleven Grammy Awards including the Grammy Trustees Award, Grammy Legend Award and the Grammy Lifetime Achievement Award.

② Perry Como
Prisoner Of Love

Label:	Written by:	Length:
Victor	Columbo / Gaskill / Robin	3 mins 14 secs

Pierino Ronald "Perry" Como (18th May 1912 - 12th May 2001) was a singer and television personality. During a career spanning more than half a century he recorded exclusively for RCA Victor after signing with the label in 1943. "Mr. C.", as he was nicknamed, sold millions of records for RCA and pioneered a weekly musical variety television show which set the standards for the genre and proved to be one of the most successful in television history.

Nat King Cole (The King Cole Trio)
(I Love You) For Sentimental Reasons

Label:	Written by:	Length:
Capitol Records	Watson / Best	2 mins 50 secs

Nathaniel Adams Coles (17th March 1919 - 15th February 1965), known professionally as Nat King Cole, was a singer who first came to prominence as a leading jazz pianist. He was widely noted for his soft baritone voice performing in big band and jazz genres. Cole was one of the first African Americans to host a national television variety show, The Nat King Cole Show, and has maintained worldwide popularity since his death in 1965.

Vaughn Monroe
Let It Snow! Let It Snow! Let It Snow!

Label:	Written by:	Length:
Victor	Jule Cahn / Sammy Styne	3 mins 3 secs

Vaughn Wilton Monroe (7th October 1911 - 21st May 1973) was a baritone singer, trumpeter, big band leader and actor whose popularity was at its height in the 1940s and 1950s. Monroe formed his first orchestra in Boston in 1940 and became its principal vocalist. He has two stars on the Hollywood Walk of Fame one for recording and one for radio.

The Ink Spots
Bless You (For Being An Angel)

Label:	Written by:	Length:
Brunswick	Don Baker / Eddie Lane	3 mins 10 secs

The Ink Spots were an African-American Pop vocal group who gained international fame in the 1930s and 1940s. The Ink Spots were widely accepted in both the white and black communities largely due to the ballad style introduced to the group by lead singer Bill Kenny. In 1989, the Ink Spots (Bill Kenny, Deek Watson, Charlie Fuqua and Hoppy Jones) were inducted into the Rock and Roll Hall of Fame and in 1999 they were inducted into the Vocal Group Hall of Fame.

Bing Crosby (& The Jesters)
Sioux City Sue

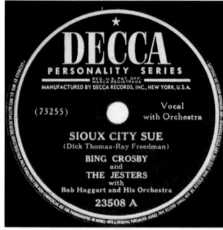

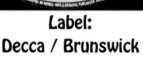

Label:	Written by:	Length:
Decca / Brunswick	Dick Thomas / Ray Freedman	2 mins 47 secs

Harry Lillis "Bing" Crosby, Jr. (3rd May 1903 - 14th October 1977) was a singer and actor. Crosby's trademark warm bass-baritone voice made him the best-selling recording artist of the 20th century having sold over one billion records, tapes, compact discs and digital downloads around the world.

Johnny Mercer
Personality

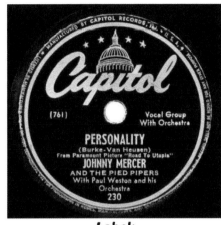

Label:	Written by:	Length:
Capitol Records	Burke / Van Heusen	2 mins 47 secs

John Herndon "Johnny" Mercer (18th November 1909 - 25th June 1976) was a lyricist, songwriter, singer and the founder of Capitol Records. From the mid-1930s through to the mid-1950s many of the songs Mercer wrote and performed were among the most popular hits of the time. He wrote the lyrics to more than fifteen hundred songs including compositions for movies and Broadway shows. He received nineteen Academy Award nominations and won four.

Eddy Howard
To Each His Own

Label:	Written by:	Length:
Majestic	Livingston / Evans	2 mins 58 secs

Edward Evan Duncan "Eddy" Howard (12th September 1914 - 23rd May 1963) was a vocalist and bandleader who was popular during the 1940s and 1950s. "To Each His Own" was the first No.1 record for Eddy Howard and his Orchestra and spent five non-consecutive weeks at the top of the pop chart in 1946. The song was a tie-in with the 1946 Paramount film, To Each His Own, which brought Academy Awards for Olivia de Havilland and screenwriter Charles Brackett.

⑨ Dinah Shore
The Gypsy

Label:
Columbia

Written by:
William Gordon Reid

Length:
2 mins 56 secs

Dinah Shore (born Frances Rose Shore; 29th February 1916 - 24th February 1994) was a singer, actress, television personality and the top-charting female vocalist during the Big Band era of the 1940s and 1950s. After failing singing auditions for the bands of Benny Goodman and both Jimmy Dorsey and his brother Tommy Dorsey, Shore struck out on her own to become the first singer of her era to achieve huge solo success.

⑩ Frankie Carle & His Orchestra
Oh! What It Seemed To Be

Label:
Columbia

Written by:
Benjamin / Carle / Weiss

Length:
2 mins 55 secs

Frankie Carle (born Francis Nunzio Carlone; 25th March 1903 - 7th March 2001) was a pianist and very popular bandleader in the 1940s and 1950s and was nicknamed "The Wizard of the Keyboard". Carle's daughter Marjorie Hughes sang with the band and was the vocalist on this record. Carle's best-known composition was "Sunrise Serenade" in 1938 which sold more than one million copies.

TOP 5
FILMS 1946

1. The Best Years Of Our Lives
2. Duel In The Sun
3. The Postman Always Rings Twice
4. Blue Skies
5. The Yearling

OSCARS

Best Film: RKO Radio Pictures
The Best Years Of Our Lives
Best Director: William Wyler
(The Best Years Of Our Lives)

Best Actor: Fredric March
(The Best Years Of Our Lives)
Best Actress: Olivia De Havilland
(To Each His Own)

THE BEST YEARS OF OUR LIVES

Directed by: William Wyler

Runtime: 172 minutes

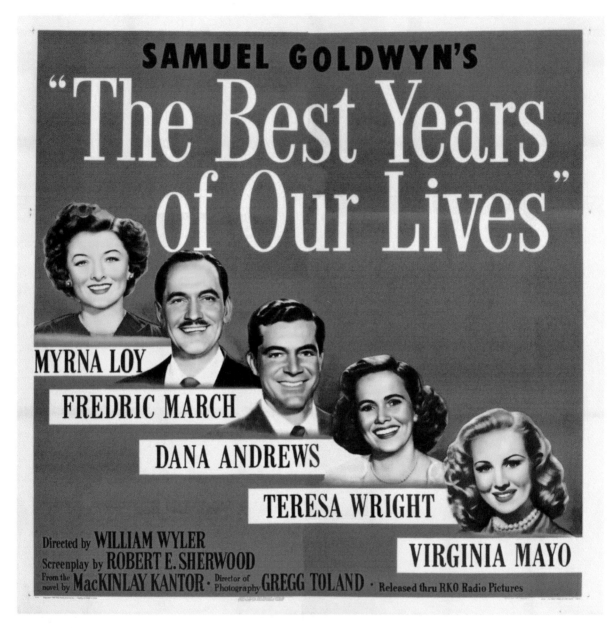

Three WWII veterans return home to small-town America to discover that they and their families have been irreparably changed.

Oscars Won:

Best Picture: Samuel Goldwyn Productions for RKO Radio Pictures
Best Actor: Fredric March
Best Dramatic or Comedy Score: Hugo Friedhofer

Best Director: William Wyler
Best Film Editing: Daniel Mandell
Best Supporting Actor: Harold Russell
Memorial Award: Samuel Goldwyn
Honorary Award: Harold Russell

Gross: $11,300,000

STARRING

Myrna Loy
Born: 2nd August 1905
Died: 14th December 1993

Character:
Milly Stephenson

Film, television and stage actress who trained as a dancer. Although originally typecast in earlier films her career took off following her portrayal of Nora Charles in The Thin Man (1934). In March 1991 Loy was presented with an Honorary Academy Award with the inscription 'In recognition of her extraordinary qualities both on screen and off, with appreciation for a lifetime's worth of indelible performances.'

Fredric March
Born: 31st August 1897
Died: 14th April 1975

Character:
Al Stephenson

A distinguished stage actor and one of Hollywood's most celebrated versatile stars of the 1930s and 1940s. He won the Academy Award for Best Actor for Dr. Jekyll and Mr. Hyde (1931) and for The Best Years of Our Lives (1946). March is the only actor to have won both the Academy Award and the Tony Award twice.

Dana Andrews
Born: 1st January 1909
Died: 17th December 1992

Character:
Fred Derry

Film actor and one of Hollywood's major stars of the 1940s who continued acting, though generally in less prestigious roles, into the 1980s. Andrews signed a contract with Samuel Goldwyn and was offered his first movie role in William Wyler's The Westerner (1940). One of his best-known roles for which he received the most praise was as war veteran Fred Derry in The Best Years of Our Lives (1946).

TRIVIA

Goofs

When Peggy makes scrambled eggs and toast for Fred she brings the eggs to the table but not the toast. The next camera shot shows Fred taking toast from the table.

When Peggy and Marie are in the ladies room at the restaurant the cameraman's left arm is visible in one of the mirrors.

At the end of the film Homer hands Fred the wedding ring and says, "Here's the ring. Don't lose it." However, his lips say, "Here's the ring. Don't drop it."

Interesting Facts

This became the most successful film at the box office since Gone with the Wind (1939) had been released 7 years earlier.

Myrna Loy receives top billing as she was the most successful female star at the time.

Interesting Facts

For his performance as Homer Parrish, Harold Russell became the only actor to win two Academy Awards for the same role. The Academy Board of Governors thought he was a long shot to win so they gave him an honorary award "for bringing hope and courage to his fellow veterans through his appearance." Later that ceremony he won Best Supporting Actor.

In a scene at Butch's bar, Homer asks Butch if he would play a song for him saying, "How about Lazy River? Remember that?" Butch, who was played by Hoagy Carmichael, actually composed "Lazy River."

In the film Fredric March's character Al Stephenson is a banker. Before becoming an actor March had a career in banking.

To avoid awkwardness when he first met his fellow cast members Harold Russell made a point of reaching out with his hooks and taking their hands thus putting them at ease with his disability.

Quote 1

Fred Derry: How long since you been home?
Al Stephenson: Oh, a couple-a centuries.

Quote 2

Milly Stephenson: What do you think of the children?
Al Stephenson: Children? I don't recognise 'em. They've grown so old.
Milly Stephenson: I tried to stop them, to keep them just as they were when you left, but they got away from me.

DUEL IN THE SUN

Directed by: King Vidor - **Runtime:** 144 minutes

Beautiful Pearl Chavez becomes the ward of her dead father's first love and finds herself torn between her sons, one good and the other bad.

Gross: $11,000,000

STARRING

Jennifer Jones
Born: 2nd March 1919
Died: 17th December 2009

Character:
Pearl Chavez

Jones was an actress during the Hollywood golden years winning the Academy Award for Best Actress for her performance in The Song of Bernadette (1943). She was also nominated for Academy Awards for her performances in four other films including as Best Actress in Duel For The Sun. Jones starred in more than twenty films over a thirty-year career and in 1980 founded the Jennifer Jones Simon Foundation For Mental Health And Education.

Joseph Cotten
Born: 15th May 1905
Died: 6th February 1994

Character:
Jesse McCanles

Film, stage, radio and television actor. Cotten achieved prominence on Broadway, starring in the original stage productions of The Philadelphia Story and Sabrina Fair. He first gained worldwide fame in the Orson Welles film Citizen Kane (1941), The Magnificent Ambersons (1942) and Journey into Fear (1943). He went on to become one of the leading Hollywood actors of the 1940s.

Gregory Peck
Born: 5th April 1916
Died: 12th June 2003

Character:
Lewton 'Lewt' McCanles

Actor who was one of the most popular film stars from the 1940s to the 1960s. Peck continued to play major film roles until the late 1970s. His performance as Atticus Finch in the 1962 film To Kill a Mockingbird earned him the Academy Award for Best Actor. He also received nominations for an Oscar in The Keys of the Kingdom (1944), The Yearling (1946), Gentleman's Agreement (1947) and Twelve O'Clock High (1949).

TRIVIA

Filming Goofs

When Jesse is sitting in his hotel room a rock flies through the window breaking the glass. As Jesse opens the window a piece of glass falls down and sticks into the lower edge of the window frame. This piece of glass disappears between shots as Jesse talks to the cowboy Sid outside.

The opening scene shows saguaro cacti in the valley. The film is supposed to take place in Texas but southern Arizona is the only place in the U.S. with saguaro cacti.

Interesting Facts

Peck's work on The Yearling overlapped for three or four weeks with Duel in the Sun. The actor would work on The Yearling in the morning and then Duel in the Sun later in the day. Describing the situation Peck reportedly said, "I didn't do much acting. I rode horses, necked with Jennifer and shot poor old Charley Bickford."

Interesting Facts   Producer & uncredited director David O. Selznick battled amphetamine addiction throughout production. His drug abuse exacerbated much of his erratic behaviour during filming including his constant demand for reshoots.

The British writing-directing team of Michael Powell and Emeric Pressburger were shown a pre-release screening of the film by producer David O. Selznick. Both were thoroughly unimpressed with the movie but didn't want to offend Selznick by saying so. At the end of the film, when Gregory Peck and Jennifer Jones are crawling towards each other on a mountain and open fire when they get near each other, Pressburger turned to Powell and whispered, "What a pity they didn't shoot the screenwriter".

Quote 1   Pearl Chavez: If I'm not good enough to marry, I'm not good enough to kiss.

Quote 2   Jesse McCanles: You mean to shoot down unarmed men?
Sen. Jackson McCanles: Just like rattlesnakes if they cross that line!

THE POSTMAN ALWAYS RINGS TWICE

Directed by: Tay Garnett

Runtime: 113 minutes

A married woman and a drifter fall in love and then plot to murder her husband, but once the deed is done they must learn to live with the consequences of their actions.

Gross: $7,600,000

STARRING

Lana Turner
Born: 8th February 1921
Died: 29th June 1995

Character:
Cora Smith

Film and television actress who was discovered in 1937 and signed by Metro-Goldwyn-Mayer aged just 16. Turner first attracted attention in They Won't Forget (1937) and during the early 1940s she established herself as a leading actress. Her popularity continued during the 1950s with films such as Peyton Place (1957) for which she was nominated for an Academy Award for Best Actress.

John Garfield
Born: 4th March 1913
Died: 21st May 1952

Character:
Frank Chambers

Actor who was adept at playing brooding, rebellious, working-class characters. In 1937 he moved to Hollywood eventually becoming one of Warner Bros.' major stars. Garfield is acknowledged as a predecessor of method actors as Marlon Brando, Montgomery Clift, and James Dean. He was nominated for the Academy Award for Best Supporting Actor for Four Daughters (1938) and Best Actor for Body and Soul (1947).

Cecil Kellaway
Born: 22nd August 1890
Died: 28th February 1973

Character:
Nick Smith

A South African-born character actor who after receiving acclaim for his main role in the Australian Cinesound film It Isn't Done (1937) was screen-tested by RKO Pictures and put under contract. During a long career as a Hollywood character actor he was twice nominated for an Academy Award for Best Supporting Actor firstly for The Luck of the Irish (1948) and then Guess Who's Coming to Dinner (1967).

TRIVIA

Goofs

When Frank and Cora first leave Nick, Cora falls in the dirt to avoid being hit by a car. All she lands on is her bottom but the dirt keeps changing its position between different shots (sometimes on her shoulders or the front of her skirt and even completely gone when she sits on the suitcase). As they are returning to the diner the dirt is back on her bottom.

At the start of the film, as the car rolls down the hill before Frank gets out, you can clearly see the crew's reflection in the side panelling of the car.

Interesting Facts

As a contrast to the fact she's playing an inherently evil character, Lana Turner wears white throughout most of the film.

The film caused a stir amongst 1940s audiences who were shocked when it seemed clear to them that John Garfield uses his tongue in one of his kissing scenes with Lana Turner.

Interesting Facts

James M. Cain (on whose book the film is based) was so impressed with Lana Turner's performance he presented her with a leather-bound copy of his book inscribed, "For my dear Lana, thank you for giving a performance that was even finer than I expected."

As originally written in the novel Madge (played by Audrey Trotter) was a lion tamer. While filming the scene in which she introduces Frank to her cats a tiger sprayed them prompting John Garfield to jokingly ask for stunt pay. The scenes involving the cats were removed and Audrey Trotters character was changed to that of a hash-house waitress.

After the first murder attempt Nick is hospitalised in Blair General Hospital which was the locale for MGM's Dr. Kildare (1961) franchise.

Quote 1

Frank Chambers: With my brains and your looks, we could go places.

Quote 2

Cora Smith: It's too bad Nick took the car.
Frank Chambers: Even if it was here we couldn't take it unless we'd want to spend the night in jail. Stealing a man's wife, that's nothing, but stealing a man's car, that's larceny.

BLUE SKIES

Directed by: Stuart Heisler

Runtime: 104 minutes

Dancer Jed loves showgirl Mary who in turn loves compulsive nightclub-opener Johnny. Unfortunately Johnny can't stay committed to anything in life for very long

Gross: $5,700,000

STARRING

Harry Lillis "Bing" Crosby Jr.
Born: 3rd May 1903
Died: 14th October 1977

Character:
Johnny Adams

An American singer and actor who from the early 1930s until the mid-1950s was a leader in record sales, radio ratings and motion picture grosses. Crosby won an Academy Award for Best Actor for his role as Father Chuck O'Malley in the film Going My Way (1944) and in 1963 he received the first Grammy Global Achievement Award. He is one of the 22 people to have three stars on the Hollywood Walk of Fame.

Fred Astaire
Born: 10th May 1899
Died: 22nd June 1987

Character:
Jed Potter

Born Frederick Austerlitz, Astaire was an American dancer, choreographer, singer, musician and actor. His stage and subsequent film and television careers spanned a total of 76 years during which he made 31 musical films and several award-winning television specials. He is best known as the dancing partner and on-screen romantic interest of Ginger Rogers.

Joan Caulfield
Born: 1st June 1922
Died: 18th June 1991

Character:
Mary O'Hara

Actress and former fashion model. After being discovered by Broadway producers she began a stage career in 1942. She had a great success portraying the troublesome teenager Corliss Archer in the 1943 hit comedy play Kiss and Tell. After a year in the role she left the production to pursue offers from Hollywood and she was replaced by her sister Betty Caulfield. For several years afterwards she was among Paramount's top stars.

TRIVIA

Anachronisms

Billy De Wolfe's character, Tony, impersonates Frankenstein's monster as a take-off of Boris Karloff during part of the movie set in the early 1920's. This was about a decade before Karloff's version of the film Frankenstein (1931) was actually produced.

Interesting Facts

Ever the perfectionist Fred Astaire spent a gruelling 5 weeks rehearsing his dance routines for the "Puttin' On the Ritz" because of the number's challenging and irregular rhythmic tempo.

Mark Sandrich, who directed several Fred Astaire and Ginger Rogers films, was the original director of Blue Skies but he died suddenly of a heart attack and was replaced by Stuart Heisler.

This was Paramount's biggest hit of 1946.

Interesting Facts   Aged 47, Fred Astaire announced his retirement after completing the film. Afterwards New York's Paramount Theatre generated a petition of 10,000 names to try to persuade him to come out of retirement. It wasn't until Gene Kelly broke his ankle though that Astaire was eventually persuaded to come back and star in the film Easter Parade (1948). He then continued to dance on in film and television until he was nearly 70.

This film was one of over 700 Paramount productions, filmed between 1929 and 1949, that were sold to Universal in 1958 for television distribution.

THE YEARLING

Directed by: Clarence Brown - **Runtime:** 128 minutes

A boy persuades his parents to allow him to adopt a young deer but what will happen if the deer misbehaves?

Gross: $5,568,000

STARRING

Gregory Peck
Born: 5th April 1916
Died: 12th June 2003

Character:
Penny Baxter

Actor whose lifetime humanitarian efforts earned him the Presidential Medal of Freedom from President Lyndon Johnson in 1969. In the 1980s Peck moved to television where he starred in the mini-series The Blue and the Gray playing Abraham Lincoln. In 1999 the American Film Institute named Peck among Greatest Male Stars of Classic Hollywood cinema ranking him at No. 12.

Jane Wyman
Born: 5th January 1917
Died: 10th September 2007

Character:
Orry Baxter

Singer, dancer, film and television actress. She began her film career in 1932 and her work in television lasted into 1993. She was nominated 4 times for the Academy Award for Best Actress (including for The Yearling), winning one of them for her performance in Johnny Belinda (1948). Wyman was a three time winner of The Golden Globe and achieved great success as Angela Channing in the 1980s prime time soap opera Falcon Crest.

Claude Jarman Jr.
Born: 27th September 1934

Character:
Jody

As a child actor Jarman was discovered in a nationwide talent search by MGM Studios and was cast as the lead actor in the film The Yearling. His performance received glowing reviews and he was awarded an Academy Juvenile Award as a result. By the time he reached his late teens MGM was finding him increasingly difficult to cast and his career was virtually over. Jarman's last film was The Great Locomotive Chase (1956).

TRIVIA

Filming Goofs

When Jody runs away from home he is barefoot. While trudging through the swamp however he is shown wearing dark gym shoes (perhaps for actual protection during filming). Later scenes show him to be barefoot again.

While Penny is cleaning his gun his bottle of oil appears, disappears and is tipped over between shots.

Interesting Facts

Marjorie Kinnan Rawlings lived and wrote the novel, The Yearling, at Cross Creek, Florida. During the movie this location was used to film some of the scenes with the rest being filmed in the Juniper Prairie Wilderness Park in the Ocala National Forest in Florida. Today there is a hiking trail named The Yearling Trail in acknowledgment of the film.

Jane Wyman's daughter refused to speak to her for two weeks after she saw the film.

Interesting Facts   Claude Jarman Jr. was chosen from over 19,000 boys to play Jody. The factor which won him the role was apparently his long hair. Jarman had been busy with school work and hadn't had a haircut in several months, which made producer Sidney Franklin think that he looked the part of a Florida farm boy.

Flag the fawn doesn't make his first appearance until one hour into the film.

Sporting Winners

1945-46 Victory Matches - Rugby

Team	Played	Won	Draw	Lost	For	Against
England	5	3	0	2	51	57
Ireland	3	0	0	3	13	24
Scotland	4	3	0	1	73	29
Wales	7	3	0	4	47	79
British Army	1	0	0	1	9	21
British Empire XV	1	1	0	0	27	6
British Empire Services	1	0	0	1	0	10

During the Second World War all international rugby matches in the UK were suspended. After the war between 1945 and 1946 a series of Victory matches were played with the Five Nations Championship resuming in 1947. The Victory matches weren't recognised as official 'capped' matches due to the absence of many players still on military service. The above table gives a summary of each team's results whilst below shows the full list of the Victory matches played (including those from 1945).

Results:

Date	Home		Score		Away	Venue
01/01/45	France		21-9		British Army	Paris
28/04/45	British Empire XV		27-6		France	Richmond
22/12/45	Wales		8-0		France	St. Helens
01/01/46	France		10-0		British Empire Services	Paris
19/01/46	Wales		13-25		England	Cardiff
26/01/46	Ireland		3-4		France	Dublin
02/02/46	Wales		6-25		Scotland	Swansea
06/02/46	England		14-6		Ireland	Twickenham
23/02/46	England		0-3		Wales	Twickenham
09/03/46	Wales		6-4		Ireland	Cardiff
16/03/46	England		12-8		Scotland	Twickenham
30/03/46	Scotland		13-11		Wales	Murrayfield
13/04/46	Scotland		27-0		England	Murrayfield
22/04/46	France		12-0		Wales	Paris

England v Scotland
16th March 1946

Result: England 12-8 Scotland

Having stood shoulder to shoulder on the battlefield, Englishmen and Scotsmen now faced-off against each other for a 'Victory' international test match at Twickenham Stadium.

MOTOR RACING - GEORGE ABECASSIS
GRANSDEN LODGE AIRFIELD GRAND PRIX

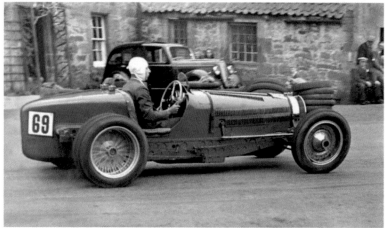 

George Edgar Abecassis aboard his Bugatti Type 59

The 1946 Gransden Lodge Grand Prix was held at Gransden Lodge Airfield near Bedford on the 15th June. Abecassis won the race in a Bugatti Type 59 during the only race meeting in England that year. At month later he took an Alta to Geneva for the prestigious Grand Prix des Nations. He qualified for the final but sadly had to retire with a failed carburettor.

SNOOKER
JOE DAVIS

The 1946 World Snooker Championship was held at the Royal Horticultural Hall in London between the 6th and 18th May and attracted a total of 14 entrants. The final was played between Horace Lindrum and defending champion Joe Davis over a marathon best of 145 frames. Davis made an unprecedented six centuries in the final including championship record breaks of 133 and 136. He only needed 7 minutes 15 seconds for the record 133 break which was also Davis' 200th century break. Davis received £1,800 for his win and Lindrum £550. Lindrum also received the championship table and all the equipment. This was Davis's 15th and last world title although he continued to play professionally until 1964.

Joe Davis   78-67   Horace Lindrum

GRAND NATIONAL
LOVELY COTTAGE

Lovely Cottage

The 1946 Grand National took place at Aintree Racecourse near Liverpool on the 5th March and was the 100th running of this world famous horse race. Lovely Cottage, a 25/1 shot trained by Tommy Rayson and ridden by jockey Captain Robert Petre, won the race by four lengths from Jack Finlay. Of the 34 horses who took part only 6 actually completed the race, 24 fell, 2 pulled up, 1 refused and 1 was brought down. This was the last Grand National to take place on a Friday, which had been the traditional day for the race since 1876.

Position	Name	Jockey	Odds
1st	Lovely Cottage	Capt. Robert Petre	25/1
2nd	Jack Finlay	William Kidney	100/1
3rd	Prince Regent	Tim Hyde	3/1

EPSOM DERBY
AIRBOURNE

Airbourne

Airbourne, an Irish-bred British-trained thoroughbred racehorse and sire, was ridden to victory by Tommy Lowrey. After showing little worthwhile form as a two-year-old Airborne improved to become one of the leading three-year-olds in Britain in 1946.

The Derby Stakes is Britain's richest horse race and the most prestigious of the country's five Classics. First run in 1780 this Group 1 flat horse race is open to three year old thoroughbred colts and fillies. It is run at Epsom Downs in Surrey over a distance of one mile, four furlongs and 10 yards (2,423 metres) and is scheduled for early June each year.

FA CUP WINNERS
DERBY COUNTY

Derby County	**4-1**	**Charlton Athletic**

Derby County   4-1   **Charlton Athletic**

Bert Turner (o.g.) 85' ⚽   ⚽ Bert Turner 86'
Peter Doherty 92' ⚽
Jackie Stamps 97' ⚽ 106' ⚽

Referee: Eddie Smith (Cumberland)

The 1946 FA Cup Final took place on the 27th April at Wembley Stadium and was attended by 98,000 spectators. The game was goalless until the 85th minute when Bert Turner managed to turn the ball into his own net. In the next minute Turner scored for his own side when he took a free-kick from the edge of the Rams' penalty area thus making him the first player to score for both sides in an FA Cup Final (and also the oldest player to score in an FA Cup Final at 36 years 312 days). When Stamps shot for goal in the closing minutes of normal time the ball burst en route to the net. Stamps went on to score twice with the new ball as Derby beat Charlton Athletic in extra time. Due to a shortage of gold following WW2 the two teams were initially presented with bronze medals. Later that year they were then awarded the proper gold versions when gold became more readily available - so effectively they were each awarded two medals for playing in the final.

THE BRITISH OPEN - GOLF

SAM SNEAD

The 1946 and 75th Open Championship was held between the 3rd and 5th July at the Old Course at St Andrews, Scotland. Sam Snead won his only Open title, the first win by an American in thirteen years and the second of Snead's seven major titles, taking the Claret Jug and prize money of £150.

The Open Championship, or simply The Open (often referred to as the British Open), is the oldest of the four major championships in professional golf and was established in 1860 at Prestwick Golf Club in Scotland. Held in the United Kingdom it is administered by The R&A and is the only major outside the United States. The winner is presented with The Golf Champion Trophy better known by its popular name of the Claret Jug.

WIMBLEDON

Mens Singles Champion - Yvon Petra - France
Ladies Singles Champion - Pauline Betz Addie - U.S.

Left Photo: Yvon Petra (left) with Geoff Brown (Australia) in the Mens Singles Final.
Right Photo: Pauline Betz Addie during a match at Wimbledon in 1946.

The 1946 Wimbledon Championships took place on the outdoor grass courts at the All England Lawn Tennis and Croquet Club in Wimbledon, London. The tournament ran from the 24th June until the 5th July and was the 60th staging of the Wimbledon Championships. In 1946 and 1947 Wimbledon was held before the French Championships and was thus the second Grand Slam tennis event of the year.

1946 CRICKET - COUNTY CHAMPIONSHIP

WINNERS:

YORKSHIRE

The County Championship is the domestic first-class cricket competition in England and Wales. The competition consists of eighteen clubs named after, and originally representing, seventeen historic counties from England and one from Wales.

Leading Run Scorer:	Laurie Fishlock	Surrey	1,963 Runs
Leading Wicket Taker:	Eric Hollies	Warwickshire	175 Wickets

THE COST OF LIVING

.. AND NOW, AS ALWAYS..
Craven 'A'
FOR YOUR THROAT'S SAKE

CARRERAS - 150 YEARS' REPUTATION FOR QUALITY

COMPARISON CHART

	1946 Price	**Equivalent Amount Today (taking into account inflation)**	**2015 Price**
3 Bedroom House	£1,900	£73,219	£209,428
Weekly Income	£4 1s 1d	£56.23	£498
Pint Of Beer	9d	£1.45	£3.31
Cheese (lb)	1s 10d	£3.53	£3.10
Bacon (lb)	2s	£3.85	£4.17
The Beano	2d	32p	£2.20

SHOPPING

Venos Cough Mixture (per bottle)	1s 4d
Beecham's Lung Syrup (large bottle)	2s 8d
Andrew Liver Salts (8oz family tin)	2s
Harrogate Health Salts (family tin)	3s 9d
Iron Jelloids	1s 4d
Atkinsons Skin Deep Beauty Cream	5s 10d
Grasshopper Ointment (for chilblains)	1s 5d
Betalax Chocolate Laxative Drops	2½d
Marmite (16oz)	4s
Weetabix (large size)	1s 1d
Bovril (2oz bottle)	1s 2d
Radox Footbath	3s 1½d
Eve Shampoo	3d
Sunlight Soap (a bar)	3d
Tek Toothbrush (nylon)	1s 10d
Gibbs Dentifrice	7½d
Lever's Easy Shaving Stick	7½d
Gumption Smooth Paste Cleanser	1s
Thorpes Washing-Up Powder (pkt)	9d
Rinso Washing Powder (large size)	7½d
Johnson's Wax Polish (large tin)	1s 8d
Kiwi Black Boot Polish (large)	8d

In the *FUTURE* — we will hold a Magic Mirror to the World —

TELEVISION! What marvels does the future hold? Colour? Pictures in vivid life-like tones? Distance? Visual transmission over thousands of miles of space? The possibilities sometimes seem too "Wellsian" to be credible. Yet one thing is certain. Whatever developments may come, Ekco who have been among the leaders of radio and television technique from the beginning, will still retain their pre-eminent position.

EKCO *Television*

E. K. COLE LTD., EKCO WORKS, SOUTHEND-ON-SEA

Other Prices

Austin 4 Door Deluxe Saloon 12HP	£531
Sodens Real Silver Fox Fur Coat	35gns
C&A Dress	£2 5s
Murphy Table Top Mains Radio (A104)	£31 11s 1d
Vacuum Cleaner	£10 16s 3d
Woodhouse 4ft Fine Quality Bedroom Suite	£47 6s 6d
Platinum Set 3 Stone Diamond Ring	£13 13s
Booths Dry Gin (bottle)	£1 5s 3d
Dewars 'White Label' Whisky (half bottle)	13s 6d
V.P. Wines (bottle)	6s 6d
Radio – Radio Rentals (per week)	1s 9d
Lessen 3 In 1 Oil (large)	2s 6d
Mahogany Tobacco (1oz)	2s 5d
Radio Times	2d

MM-MM!
THEY'VE DELICIOUS CHOCOLATE COATING

MM-MM!
THEY'VE MUNCHY MALT HONEYCOMB CENTRES

Mm-mm . . . much more to munch in
Maltesers

The POWDER with the extra C-L-I-N-G

OUTDOOR GIRL
OLIVE OIL POWDER

Yes

Coca-Cola

 *Maintaining the Breed*

Decendant of a family of thoroughbreds, the T.C. Series Midget
Possesses all the stamina and resilience of its predecessors. Easy to handle,
with lively power, rapid acceleration and lightning response to controls.
Price £375.0.0d. ex Works (plus purchase Tax £104.18.4)

Safety Fast!

THE MG CAR COMPANY LTD., ABINGDON-ON-THAMES, BERKS

THE MONEY

Money Conversion Table

Old Money		Equivalent Today
Farthing	¼d	0.1p
Half Penny	½d	0.21p
Penny	1d	0.42p
Threepence	3d	1.25p
Sixpence	6d	2.5p
Shilling	1s	5p
Florin	2s	10p
Half Crown	2s 6d	12.5p
Crown	5s	25p
Ten Shillings	10s	50p
Pound	20s	£1
Guinea	21s	£1.05

Huntley & Palmers

John Ginger

The first name you think of in Biscuits

Printed in Great Britain
by Amazon